COFFEE-TIME PRAYERS

Lynn Sallee

BAKER BOOK HOUSE
Grand Rapids, Michigan

To
LORRY

my husband
my partner
my friend

ISBN: 0-8010-8083-5

Printed in the United States of America

Contents

1

That First Cup of Coffee

I stirred up the pancake batter as I wrote out a check for lunch money. The sizzling cakes and perking coffee accompanied shrill voices arguing about whose turn it was to get on the school bus first. "What shirt matches these pants?" my bare-chested husband came downstairs to ask. So leaving the orange juice half mixed, I went up to choose an outfit for him. Back to the juice and then the dog had to go out. Daughter was protesting that her brother had tied knots in her shoelaces and son needed a button sewed on.

8:05 and all is quiet. Husband off to work, kids on the school bus, and dog dozing under the table—at last I have time for that first cup of coffee.

GOOD MORNING, LORD. A new day has dawned and I thank You for every harried minute of it. Now in this brief but much appreciated moment of leisure and solitude, be with me. Stimulate and refresh me with Your Word and Spirit. Grant me the strength, stamina, and serenity I need to cope with today's tasks.

2

Thinning the Carrots

I'm not one to waste seeds. If my vegetable garden has room for only two fifteen-foot rows of carrots, I still manage to sprinkle two packets of seeds into the neatly drawn furrows. "You have to plan on some bad seeds," I explain to my husband, trying to justify my action. A few weeks later I'm rewarded with rows packed with tiny green plants. (My seeds always seem to have 100 percent germination!)

"You'll have to thin them out," my husband says. Reluctantly, I pull up one seedling here, another there. "Not like that—like this!" and he grabs whole handfuls of my lovely new plants and yanks them out. "They have to have room to grow."

FATHER, my life sometimes gets as crowded as the carrot plants in my vegetable garden. And I know that I need room to grow, too. But it's so difficult sometimes to say no, to keep from getting too involved. Help me to thin out the garden of my life. Show me how to weed out the unnecessary surpluses so that the really valuable part of me can expand and enlarge. Guide me toward my own little plot of ground where I can receive the water of Your love and the nourishment of Your grace.

3

Caught Up in the Blues

Nothing has gone right all day. The sun has stayed hidden under gray clouds, afraid to peek out. One of the kids announced he just couldn't go to school because his throat was sore, his stomach ached, and his nose was plugged up. Fifteen minutes after the bus chugged past he suddenly felt well enough to get up and watch Captain Kangaroo. I ran out of coffee, but I can't leave my child home alone while I run to the store for another can. Then the zipper broke on my new jeans. Most days these petty annoyances wouldn't bother me much at all. I'd be able to shrug them off and get on with my activities. But today I'm caught up in the blues—today everything is a major catastrophe.

FATHER, I don't know why I have these blue days. I just feel dissatisfied and restless. None of my usual activities capture my interest. Even taking a day off from housework for my hobbies doesn't hold much fascination. I'm as blah and gray as the weather.

Won't You help me shake off this down-in-the-dumps mood? Time is so precious that I shouldn't waste even one hour of it moping around. Remind me of all my blesssings, of all the good things in my life. Maybe if I count my blessings instead of my grievances the gray fog will dissolve and my blues will be replaced with sunshine.

4

These Unwanted Children

My daily newspaper reports all the nauseating stories of abused and neglected children. A 6-month-old baby abandoned in a garbage can. A 10-year-old boy hung by his wrists from a door frame until he died from starvation. A curly-haired little girl hideously scarred by the burns her father inflicted with his cigarette lighter. A bruised and battered boy brought into the emergency room after his mother "punished" him for refusing to clean his plate. I read these stories but I have trouble believing them. What parent could treat his own young child so cruelly?

YOU WHO ARE the Father of all these unwanted children must hear their cries of fear, their screams of pain. But why do You ignore the prayers of these innocent young children? I'm frustrated with Your seeming abandonment of them. I can do nothing to help them—but You can. What is the purpose of their suffering? What conceivable good could grow out of their agony? Your Son Jesus told us, "Let the little children come to me." I commend all of these unwanted children to You today. Please, Father, I plead that You'll gather them to You and wrap them in Your loving protection.

5

Run, Mom, Run

The alarm clock jars me from sleep. Dragging myself out from the comforting warmth of bed, I don my baggy sweatpants, fluorescent orange hooded sweatshirt, Adidas jogging shoes, and strap on a watch with second hand. Then out in the cool morning air to begin a mile of torture. Panting, wheezing, trying to shake a cramp out of my left calf without pausing, I race the sweep second hand back to the front door. Drenched with perspiration I hurry into the house to mark my labors in the daily log: Tuesday, 7:45 AM, 1 mile, time: 11:35. No, I'm never going to set any records in my quest for physical fitness—not with a sub-12-minute mile!

LORD, I've not done much with my body in all these years since childhood. It's weak and tires easily. But now, for the first time, I know the exhilaration of pushing it to the limit, of reaching and struggling to my full capacity. It's a tremendously satisfying feeling. Each day I'm stronger and faster than the day before. My muscles respond better and my heart and lungs can work harder. Aren't You pleased to see that I've finally realized the value of making the body You gave me a strong and healthy one?

But, Father, I'm still lazy at heart. I still find it difficult to leave my bed and face another mile. Won't You give me the moral strength to continue working toward physical fitness? Help me put forth that extra effort when my children stand at the driveway, one eye on the watch and the other on my slowly approaching figure, shouting, "Run, mom, run!"

6

Just Floating in the Water

There's no feeling that quite compares to the total relaxation of floating in the water on a beautiful summer afternoon. Buoyed up by the water, I don't have to put any effort into staying afloat. And the stillness found when my ears sink below water level is unique and unexplainable. It's more than the absence of noise, it's the presence of quiet. One has to experience it personally to appreciate the sensation. What a delicious break for frazzled nerves!

FATHER, help me to learn the art of floating in the waters of life. Teach me how to release my body, mind, and soul to Your will. Then I won't have to thrash around aimlessly in this world for I will have the support I need to keep me afloat. Buoyed up by Your grace and love, perhaps I can find the same sensations of peace and quiet that I find just floating in the water.

7

Thank You for My Husband

He never buys me candy or flowers and seldom remembers my birthday or Valentine's Day. He turns on the lights when I try to surprise him with a candlelight dinner because he claims he can't find his food in the dark. For Christmas he gives me nice practical gifts like a solder iron or an apple corer. My husband doesn't have one romantic bone in his body!

We don't have much in common either. He's as quiet as I am boisterous. I like fishing and football while he collects old plates and tends the rose garden. I read only murder mysteries and he reads only science fiction. But more important than all our differences is one vital fact: After more than a decade of marriage we still mean it when we say, "I love you."

FATHER, I thank You for this fine husband who shares my life. He's a kind and giving man. While

he might forget to buy me a Valentine, he might also dig me a dozen worms for fishing or volunteer to wash dishes or walk the dog. He shows his love in more personal ways than the traditional box of candy—more personal and therefore more precious.

I thank You, too, that he's a good father to our children. He can be patient with them when I can't. He takes time to be with them and enjoy them. They are learning a great deal about the goodness of life from his example.

Today I come to You as a wife asking that You'll bless this man who shares my life and owns my heart. Help us to walk hand in hand down the road of life You map out for us, alive in Your grace and our love for each other.

8

Women I Will Never Meet

More than a billion women inhabit the earth today. Scattered across the globe, many live in societies and cultures far different from mine. Few enjoy the affluence and freedom that I do. And of all these millions and millions of women who are my sisters, I will probably never know more than a few hundred.

FATHER, I pray today for all the women I will never meet. They may be unfamiliar and unknown to me but they are not strangers to You. You alone know their needs and desires, for You alone have the power to look into their hearts. Many of them will come to You in prayer today just as I have. Some will speak to You from desperation and hopelessness. Won't You hear their prayers and bless them with an answer to their questions?

9

America: Love It or Leave It

America the beautiful isn't quite as lovely as it once was. Pollution and land waste have taken their toll. Inflation and unemployment rear their ugly heads. The scars of government corruption and political assassinations still disfigure. Crime and violence, poverty and prejudice—we pay a heavy price for these, too.

No, America is not so beautiful anymore because *Americans* are not so beautiful. We're consumer hogs—gobbling up more than our share of the world's food and natural resources. We are materialistic to the point that lofty words like *morality*, *integrity*, and *ethics* give way to a third car and a second bathroom. Once a great showcase for democracy, we have become a source of ridicule and scorn. Once a nation under God, we have allowed the almighty dollar to become our god.

FATHER, please do not lose faith in America or Americans. We live in troubled times now, but one of the unique characteristics of Americans is that they can endure the bad times and come out stronger and wiser. This is a time for setting new goals and directions, a time for self-examination. I pray that You'll provide all Americans, but specially those who hold high office, with the wisdom to learn from past mistakes and the strength to alter our course at whatever personal sacrifice.

Finally, Father, I pray for the young. They are the hope and the future of our country. Are You as encouraged as I am by what You see of them? Many possess the idealism and vision of their forefathers. A great many have transferred their allegiance from the dollar sign back to You. Guide these young adults so that they can make America and the world a far better place than the legacy we leave to them.

10

Cutting Out a Dress Pattern

The length of fabric, carefully folded with right sides together, covers my dining room table. I've assembled the assorted paraphernalia I'll need: pins, shears, pattern, dressmaker's carbon. Now comes the most trying part of sewing for me—getting all the pattern pieces positioned on the fabric. I don't know why I always seem to have 1⅞ yards of material when the pattern calls for 2¼!

FATHER, my life is just one big dress pattern. Like that too short piece of fabric, I scrimp and save and make do with the minimum. I don't have any more giving or loving left over than I do fabric scraps when I finish cutting out a pattern. Help me to enlarge the fabric of my life, to become more generous in my allowances of love for You and my fellow human beings.

In cutting out my dress pattern, I have to use all the pieces. I can't just omit any piece that won't fit. I can't discard a collar or sleeve or shorten a skirt at will without ruining the whole effect of the finished garment. Remind me that neither can I omit any opportunity to do good in this world. Not if I want my soul to fit!

11

They're Getting a Divorce

Over a cup of coffee this morning, my good friend confided that she and her husband had filed for divorce. Was I surprised? No, I guess not really. They hadn't been happy together for several years. Counseling hadn't helped them salvage their marriage despite their genuine efforts to stay together because of their young children. At last the final break has come. Each will now travel on a separate path, building a new life alone—but intersecting now and then in the interests of their youngsters.

My friend is torn by emotions. Bitterness over a dead love that no amount of effort was able to revive. Insecure and afraid of a future alone. But, most of all, lonely. She has no one to confide in, share with, cry with, laugh with. Life for a divorced person, I realized, must be awfully bleak and barren.

FATHER, help me learn from my friend's heartbreak. Love is a delicate and fragile flower that needs tending to grow and blossom. Like the flower, too, it is only beautiful if it is alive and healthy. Remind me to water my own garden of love often with tender words and gentle touches.

Thank You for a marriage that is strong and

vigorous—and for a husband who shares my desire to keep our love growing. I pray that we'll never take the blessing of our happy union for granted and let it wither and die from want of care.

If we ever do have serious troubles, I hope we'll remember to come first to You for counseling. You can see into both our hearts and show us the way to reconcile any differences. Relying on Your help, Lord, I pray that my husband and I will never know the heartbreak of divorce.

12

Stained-Glass Windows

The soft glow of violet and amber and turquoise. The more vivid accents of ruby and orange. Stained-glass windows enchant me. Sometimes, I confess, I study them so deeply during Sunday service that the sermon flies over my head unnoticed. But there's a fascination to old stained-glass windows with their Tiffany bull's-eyes and well-aged lead caming that can block out the rest of my surroundings. Inscriptions from long ago reveal a window's age, it's true, but a more telling story can be found in the cracks and repairs and not-quite-matching glass section replacements. These relics of the past have been loved and cared for by generations of past church members whose efforts preserved them for me to enjoy every Sunday morning.

FATHER, several years ago I read a message about stained-glass windows that I've often remembered since. I can't recall the exact words but it read something like this: "People are like stained-glass windows. They sparkle and glow when the sun is bright; but when the sun goes down, their beauty is revealed only if there is a light within." It's the light of Your spirit shining in us that gives us beauty even when everything around us is dark and forbidding. Help me to serve as Your stained-glass window—reflecting Your light clearly for all the world to see.

13

Who Am I?

"You must be Kelly's mother," the smiling teacher said, extending a hand, as we met for parent-teacher conference.

"Are you Lorry's wife?" asked the girl next to me at the company Christmas party.

"Are you 582-7489?" the telephone operator queried.

I wanted to shout no. And neither am I Social Security Number 392-42-5226. Nor the 4-H leader. Nor the "lady in the red VW bus," as the grocery carry-out boy insists. I'm *me*, a person with a name of my own. Doesn't anybody know or care?

LORD, who am I? Am I only somebody's mother, somebody's wife, a telephone number, a Social Security number? I come to You today because maybe You are the only one who knows me as a separate, distinct, unique person. You know the goodness and the evil that coexist within me. You alone, Father, really know my name.

I'm urgently searching for an identity. It's not enough for me to be an extension of anyone else or a convenient number. I have to know my own worth, my own direction in life, my own inner self. Please help me, Father, to sort out my many faces and facades and come to know the real me. Help me find an answer to that very difficult question, "Who am I?"

14

What Are Neighbors For?

Yesterday morning I ran out of flour as I was making bread. Cup in hand, I walked to the house across the road and apologetically asked the elderly lady who lives there if I could borrow a cup of flour. "Here, take the whole sack," she said, thrusting it into my hands. "Just return what you don't use."

"I'm really sorry to bother you, but I can't afford to waste all the ingredients I've already mixed," I explained. "You know how it is with yeast breads. . . ."

"Don't give it a thought," she interrupted. "What are neighbors for?"

I don't know how many times I've borrowed from this friendly, generous woman in the eight years we've lived across the road from her. An egg, a bottle of Worcestershire sauce, clothespins, a card table and folding chairs—she's loaned them all willingly. And every time I come asking, she answers with the same question, "What are neighbors for?"

FATHER, this woman's generation has something valuable to teach my generation—something I'm afraid we've forgotten in our modern emphasis on every man for himself. She knows the fine art of being a good neighbor. She gives of herself freely, she shares her possessions cheerfully, and she finds genuine pleasure in helping others. I pray, perhaps selfishly, that You'll bless her with many more years so she can remain our much-needed example of a value we sometimes think obsolete—neighborliness. She reminds me that, yes, I *am* my brother's keeper. In our materialistic and self-centered society, that's one reminder well worth repeating.

15

I'm So Tired

All day I've felt rushed. So much work to do and so few hours to do it. Experts say the American housewife (thanks to machines and labor-saving tools) has a soft life. I don't believe it! Not after running up and down the stairs with baskets of laundry all morning. My vacuum cleaner may be a great invention but it isn't advanced enough to run around the carpets by itself. Even if I owned every labor-saving device on the market, I'd still have to empty the garbage, clean the toilet bowl, change the bed sheets, shampoo the kids' hair, mend the hole in my husband's pants, set the table for dinner, and then cook the meal.

It's been a long, long time since breakfast. I've accomplished a great deal already today but a lot more remains to be done. And I'm so tired!

FATHER, I'm physically tired. I ache right down to my bones with longing for a nap. My bed invites but my work holds me back. But worse than the physical tiredness is the spiritual slumber I've fallen into. I'm too numb with fatigue to share any part of myself with You. Please forgive me for my indifference today. I'll try to be wide awake for You tomorrow, but right now I'm just too tired.

16

Help Me Listen

I overheard a group of boys on the playground this afternoon. Four boys all chattering at once. One was telling about the new puppies at his house. Another was extolling the virtues of his sneakers. A third was discussing the Packer-Viking game, and the fourth was complaining about a homework assignment. I chuckled because it was obvious that while all four were talking, no one was listening.

O LORD, how much like those small boys I am. I'm so busy asking You to give me this or spare me from that, that I never take time to listen to You. I cannot hear because I'm never quiet long enough for You to get a word in edgewise. Remind me often that prayer can be a passive, receptive moment in my day. Help me clear my mind from distraction and suppress my own desires and needs long enough for You to speak to me. Teach me, Father, to be a good listener.

17

Bless My Mother

"I'll show you how to fly it. I was kite flying champion in grade school." The first hints of spring invariably meant my mother would confiscate my kite with the stated purpose of teaching me how to fly it. Just as invariably it would end up dangling from utility wires or tangled in a tree with the first stiff breeze.

Of all the thousands of things a mother teaches her daughter, the most worthwhile thing my mother taught me was how to enjoy life, how to have fun, how to make every minute count. She wasn't afraid of what the neighbors would say if she glided around the ice with us, notoriously weak ankles tightly strapped in a vain atempt to keep them from rolling inward or outward. She didn't hesitate to fly down a snowy hill in a metal saucer. And I can't count how many marshmallow roasts and sing-alongs around a bonfire she led for my sister and me and all our friends on summer evenings. Or how about a wiener roast in the middle of a January snowstorm?

My mother—zany, happy, impulsive, filled to the brim and overflowing with life—what an example she was to two growing daughters. How much richer our adult lives are for learning how to enjoy all life has to offer!

FATHER, please bless my mother with many more winters of ice skating and springs of kite flying. The new pair of ice skates she bought this fall are a sure sign that her grandchildren will re-peat some of the happy experiences I remember from my youth.

Remind me, too, Lord, that my mother taught me many lessons I didn't really learn until I viewed them from an adult perspective. She did and still does live life to the fullest but she also worked and sacrificed for her family. Her life wasn't all games and play—it just seemed that way to her children. Perhaps that's the highest compliment a daughter can pay her mother—that she always found time to teach her children how to live. You, who must find time for all Your children, must be very proud of her.

18

My Aloneness

Someone recently wrote that the greatest problem of modern man is that he can't spend an hour alone in a room. I find that idea so sad. People who can't be alone with themselves never find the blessings that silence and solitude can bring. But I know that I fit into that definition of modern man to some extent. I can become so wrapped up in work, family, social life, and recreation that I don't find time to be alone. It's not that I shun solitude—but I don't always search for it either.

LORD, every man is an island, isn't he? We come into the world alone and we leave it alone. Even along life's journey we may walk alongside someone, but we still walk alone.

Sometimes I'm frightened by my aloneness. I forget that even if I walk alone among men, You are still with me. I'm grateful that You'll never desert me, Father; that I'll never experience that true aloneness one feels when he loses the sense of the presence of God.

19

I'm Afraid

Am I the only grown woman in the world who needs a night light? Sometimes I think I must be when I hear about all the business and hunting and fishing trips other women's husbands take. Surely none of those wives share my terrible fear of the dark. None of them become frightened when the sun sets and they are alone in the house. They don't push chairs under door knobs or lie in bed awake listening intently to every creak and squeak. I envy those women because they don't know my fear of something I can't escape. They'll never know the weakness and dependence that such a fear brings with it.

FATHER, maybe other women don't share my phobia of the dark but some do share the knowledge of fear. Among my friends is one girl absolutely terrified of birds and another afraid of storms. Their fears may take a different form but we share the anger and frustration of dealing with our irrational fears.

I pray, Lord, that You'll view with compassion all of us who are afraid. Help us to deal with our fears—to face them, accept them, and then have the strength and courage to overcome them. Remind us to put our trust in You when our emotions become too great to handle alone.

20

Who Cares About Cobwebs?

It was my turn as hostess of the women's club and I'd cleaned the house from top to bottom. Floors shone with slick coats of wax, all dog hairs were vacuumed off the upholstery, the knick-knacks were washed and polished until they sparkled in the light. My best china and silver were laid out and I'd baked a fancy dessert. Then during the meeting, one of the members stood to give a report and reached up to pull loose a gigantic cobweb hanging from the ceiling. Frantically looking around the room, I quickly found dozens more hiding in corners and draping the ceiling. The only thing I'd forgotten was those pesky cobwebs!

FATHER, I don't ask You to make me a meticulous housekeeper. You can work miracles, I know; but my faith isn't big enough to comprehend a miracle of that magnitude. I only ask that you make me a little more aware of dirt and disorder. My laissez-faire attitude toward cobwebs (if-you-don't-bother-me-I-won't-bother-you) may cause the spider population to bless me but it certainly doesn't demonstrate good housekeeping practices. Help me become more than a swipe and wipe cleaner.

But I also thank You that I'm not so fussy about my house that it ceases to be a home. I want my family and friends to feel comfortable and welcome here. Help me find the middle of the road: just enough cobwebs to look like a home, but not so many that my living room becomes a zoologist's paradise!

21

Just Sign Me Ms.

I'm just a little bit confused by the new termi-
nology to grow out of the Equal Rights Amend-
ment. Oh, I can understand the new, all-inclusive
abbreviation Ms. That's really elementary. But I
keep forgetting to change chairman to chairperson
in the club's minutes. And I'm totally bewildered
when it comes to using only neuter pronouns.
"He/she" or "(s)he" seems too stiff and "that person" or "the one who" is awkward. "He" and
"she," "his" and "hers" seemed like perfectly valid
words in the English language—but women's lib
virtually wiped them out of the dictionary!

FATHER, I agree and identify with the women's
liberation movement. Equal rights and equal
opportunity should be everyone's birthright. Isn't
that what Your Son Jesus came down to earth to
teach us? But now, nearly two thousand years later,
many of us are still trying to grasp the implications
of His life and teachings. We're slow learners,
aren't we?

But caught up in the fervor of a movement that's
right and just, we always seem to descend to the
absurd and trivial. We lose sight of the larger goals
and objectives. Whether to use "chairman" or
"chairperson" becomes more important than the
fact that we've never had a woman president. Help
us—both men and women—to take a larger view,
to fight only those battles that may win the war
against discrimination.

I pray, too, that my sisters and I, in the first flushes of victory, will not forget others whose cause is urgent. Man, the aged, racial and religious minorities also deserve equal rights and opportunities. Remind us to use our freedom to aid others in gaining theirs.

Finally, Father, I ask You to remind us that rights and opportunity may be given but success, dignity, and respect must be earned. No signature on a bill can provide them for us. Help women to use the liberation movement as a springboard to grow, to become, to achieve.

22

On Our Anniversary

Candlelight, lasagna, a toast, and just the two of us for our anniversary dinner.

"You put green peppers in the lasagna again," my husband accused, lifting a noodle with his fork to poke suspiciously through the meat and cheese filling below.

"Just a little," I confessed, "and I chopped it up real fine. I really didn't think you'd notice."

A long sigh was his only answer. Who wants to start an argument on your anniversary? Another futile attempt to educate his palate. Clinging to the theory that if you eat something often enough you get to like it, I've touted oatmeal, green peppers, mushrooms, and dried prunes since the day we married. But I'm beginning to admit my husband had a valid point when he viewed his oatmeal at breakfast the other morning and asked, "If I haven't gotten to like this mush in the last eleven years, what on earth makes you think I'll get to like it in the next eleven?"

FATHER, this day which marks the end of another year of marriage is a cause for celebration. With the soaring divorce rates, just being together at the end of another year can make us both grateful for your guidance in this area of our lives. And coming to an anniversary still happy and in love is truly one of the greatest blessings You've bestowed on us. Thank You for sustaining us this far on our marital journey.

Help me in the coming year to finally accept the inevitable—that my husband is never going to change. He'll always like ultraconservative clothes and hide the blue, pink, and chartreuse flowered shirt I gave him for Christmas in the back of the closet. No amount of explanations of the nutritional value of oatmeal is going to alter his opinion of the cereal. These differences are so minor, so trivial, that surely I can learn to make allowances —just as he acknowledges my dislike of liver. Remind me often in the next 365 days that I love him for what he is, not what he wears or eats.

An anniversary marks the end of one year but also the beginning of the next. Please bless both my husband and me with the determination to continue growing and building together in the year and all the years ahead.

23

As the White Bass Run. . .

I have a quiet fishing spot where other fishermen seldom come. It's a little bridge alongside a woods on a sparsely traveled country road. Perhaps the reason no one else fishes there is that the inhabitants of that stretch of river are extremely finicky eaters. I can tempt them with the most plump, juicy nightcrawler, but those stubborn fish just swim around the hook and skeptically view my bait.

Why do I go back to that fishing hole day after day when everyone else with rod and pole is down the river four miles pulling in one white bass after another? Part of the reason is the beauty and solitude of the area. But a big part, I confess, is that when those fish finally decide to bite they really seem ravenous. Both corks will start bobbing at the same time, then a jerk, and a fish takes off with the bait he'd ignored for hours. Within a short time I fill my stringer and rush home to clean my catch for supper. Patience pays off with a meal of white bass!

FATHER, I often worship You more meaningfully when I'm fishing than when I'm in church. This little stretch of river where I can be alone with You and nature serves as my weekday cathedral.

My husband once told me he didn't think I cared whether or not I caught anything—I just liked the fishing. Maybe that's true. The world slows down on the riverbank, and I slow down, too. I have time for You as I watch the bobbers floating across the ripples, time I seldom find to give You from my busy day. So if You have something important to tell me, won't You save it for my next fishing trip—but please don't bring it up just when those finicky fish finally decide to bite!

24

No Raving Beauty

My friends, family, even my husband might lie; but the mirror doesn't. The face it reflects back at me is never going to win a beauty contest or cause any man with 20/20 vision to stop on the street and stare. I like to think it has character; but in truth, it only features a mouth too full, a jawline too square, a high forehead, and a brown mole on the right cheek. Oh, I try to make the most of what I've got. Shading along the cheeks makes my face look more rounded. Bangs cover my high forehead. And my hair is cut short to show off the tiny, well-formed ears which are my only great asset. But even with all my cosmetic tricks, I'm never going to be any raving beauty!

LORD, I'm thankful that my lack of physical beauty isn't important to You. You look deeper, far beneath the eyeshadow and contour creams. You give all of us—beautiful, ugly, and just average—an equal start in the quest for Your favor.

I hope when You look into my soul You find more beauty than I find when I look into the mirror. The blemishes or imperfections You find there are so much more serious than the mole on my cheek that causes me anxiety. Help me to pay as much attention to my spiritual appearance as I do to my physical appearance. Remind me that an ugly soul cannot be covered up with cosmetics!

25

Tears of Joy, Tears of Sorrow

I come from a long line of criers. Back in my younger years, mom and my sister and I gathered around a box of Kleenex when we watched a sad television show. Now my daughter and I share the tissue carton when viewing the tear jerkers. I spent a whole rainy afternoon crying as I read *Love Story*. The pages got so damp I had to weight the book down until it dried (the library doesn't appreciate a returned book with curled pages)!

FATHER, thank You for providing me with a full range of emotions. I cry easily over a sad movie or book, it's true, but I also find the release of tears when trouble and grief overwhelm me. Those tears cleanse and heal as well as relieve the pressure of bottled-up feelings.

I thank You, too, that You've given me the blessing of laughter. Life is so much richer when we can laugh at ourselves—at all our foibles and foolishness. When I begin to take myself or my problems too seriously, remind me that laughter puts people and things in their true perspective.

Lord, if I could ask just one blessing for all people on earth it would be the gift of tears and laughter. I'd ask it for all those solemn-faced people who've forgotten how to laugh, for all the males who never learned to cry because "men don't cry," for all those persons whose tear ducts are dry because they don't know how to feel or care. For with tears and laughter comes a completeness of personality, a rounding out of character that makes for more caring, loving people. Isn't that what the world needs now?

26

Over the Back Fence

"Come on over for coffee this morning," my friend invites me over the phone. "Have I got a piece of gossip for you!" I drop my dust mop and hang up the dish towel, leaving my work unfinished for the chance to hear a juicy tidbit of news.

Which of my friends or acquaintances is getting a divorce, got snared in a scandal, or needs psychiatric care? Whose IUD failed? Who beat up her child or got beaten up by her husband? Who signed up for food stamps? Whose child sniffed glue? Whose husband got fired from his job? The range of gossip is virtually limitless.

FATHER, I should be ashamed of myself for my eagerness to hear a piece of gossip. Someone's reputation will be damaged, perhaps unjustly, by a rumor that started from a small spark and spreads like a crown fire from house to house throughout the community. I'm worried that I so seldom remember that listening to or spreading gossip is wrong. Please prod my lazy conscience more often so I become aware of the harm my idle chatter might do to someone else.

Give me the strength of character not to repeat any scandal I hear. Not to my husband or best friend or (especially) the girls in my neighborhood Bible study class. It's so tempting to share the secret with just one person—but that's the way the fire of rumor is fed.

Finally, Father, I ask that You show me the way to turn any ugly gossip I hear into an offer of help and hope. If a friend has a drinking problem, mistreats her child, or is mentally ill, help me find time to offer whatever help I can. Could I babysit for her child a few afternoons to help relieve the tension between them? Could I offer a willing ear and a cup of coffee if she needs someone to talk to? Let me respond to another's needs when I become alerted to them by chatter over the back fence.

27

Oh, No, the Market's Falling!

Alcoa 44⅛, off 1¼; Standard Oil of New Jersey 29½, off ⅝; Polaroid 67¼, off 2⅛. Another bad day on Wall Street as Big Board prices drop one more rung on the financial ladder. The Dow-Jones averages plummet steadily downward.

My own small investments—not a blue chip among them—are following the trend established by the industrial giants. Every day at market closing my stock certificates are worth a little less than the day before. Why? Maybe a rumor of a steel shortage, maybe the prime interest rate rose half a percentage point, maybe the president sneezed twice. Who knows the answer?

And tomorrow the same stocks may reverse and begin an upward trend for an equally elusive reason or no reason at all. The world of Wall Street is fickle and unpredictable, despite all the highly touted newsletters which claim ability to pick the winners.

FATHER, I find that life is so very much like the stock market. Sometimes I'm rising and sometimes I'm falling—and I don't always know the reason for my direction. Like Wall Street, I seem to be controlled by an unseen power that decides my course. You, I know, are that unseen power in my life. Help me to accept Your guidance even when I don't understand the reason behind it. Give me the strength to endure the pain and unhappiness that comes with the lows. And remind me to thank You when You bless me with a steady upward trend or a new yearly high.

28

No Two Snowflakes Just Alike

Scientists tell us that no two of all the zillions of fluffy white snowflakes that fall in a winter are exactly the same. I look out my window at the huge drifts piled up on the lawn and find myself questioning the scientists' findings. Surely in all those heaps. . . .

I bundle up and go outside to conduct my own research. Snowflakes flutter down and land on my jacket sleeve. Quickly I compare them in that brief instant before they dissolve into dampness. I've repeated my experiment every winter since I was a small child. I've never found two identical snowflakes—but I keep searching.

FATHER, it's hard for me to accept that all in nature is unique. Each passing season brings miracles distinctly different from any that preceded or any that will follow. And like the snowflakes that are never alike, people, too, are uniquely themselves. As different as their fingerprints, they defy classification and labeling. But like my snowflake experiment, I keep trying to pin labels on people, to fit them into little boxes. I forget to appreciate their very differentness and to marvel at the diversity of Your creation.

Help me to appreciate each person I meet for his own special qualities. Help me to see that each of us fills a special niche in Your great plan. Mysterious are Your ways, Lord, but none is as mysterious to me as the miracle that makes each new baby coming forth from his mother's body a totally unique being. I feel very small and unimportant in view of this infinity of distinctness.

41

29

Thank You for My Father

Today when every magazine I open carries an article titled "What's a Father?" or "How to Be a Good Father" or "How a Busy Father Can Find Time for His Children," I chuckle and look back to my own childhood. My father didn't need any set of instructions on how to be a parent. The guidelines were printed in his heart.

My dad has taught me so many things that have shaped my life and made me the person I am today. Little things like how to make potato pancakes or catch a jumbo perch, but also bigger things we sometimes call values. Unfortunately, not all of his examples rubbed off on me. He's a perfectionist whether the task at hand is washing dishes or carving a gun stock, while I've adopted the "get it done quickly and halfway decently" attitude. And maybe a few of the character traits I've inherited, like my extremely competitive nature, I'd be better off without. (A game of badminton in our family has been accurately dubbed Civil War II.) But looking back to the whole of dad's influence on my growing up years, I realize now that while he wasn't perfect or infallible, I was fortunate to have him for my father.

YOU, who are my heavenly Father, must surely appreciate the tremendous task my father faced in

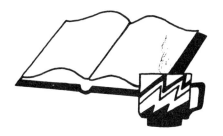

being my parent. I wasn't an easy child to cope with, was I? Stubborn, lazy, independent, without an ounce of common sense or tact. Did You and he sometimes despair that I would ever grow up to find a niche in this world? Together You guided me to adulthood and, while I certainly didn't always appreciate Your joint effort then, now I can offer a sincere thank you to you both.

Please bless my father, Lord, with the peace and contentment that comes when a difficult job is finished. Reward him with many more years to enjoy his grandchildren and share in their growing up. And remind him when his granddaughter beats him in a bitterly fought game of Monopoly, that some part of him lives on in yet another generation!

30

Why Can't Women Get Along?

This month's meeting of the women's club differed little from last month or the month before that. It's amazing to me what minor matters we women can find to bicker about—whether to donate $5 or $10 to the Art Appreciation Fund, whether the new meeting room curtains should be of antique satin or if a heavy cotton would do, whether the Ways and Means Committee really needs eight members or if six would be enough.

It's bad enough that we must argue and tempers flare up over these trivialities, but even worse is the whispered back-stabbing and outright attacks on each other. When a new member was introduced this evening, the girl next to me leaned over and whispered, "Oh, goodee, just what we need! She's so bossy that she drove the other PTA officers up the wall when she was secretary." From the next table I overheard snatches of conversation as eight women hashed over another member's continual tiffs with her in-laws. Who, I wondered, was paying any attention to the business meeting going on?

FATHER, don't You get discouraged when You look down on us and witness only discord? I am ashamed of my sisters when we show that we can't get along with each other. Surely You who created us must be even more disheartened than me. Do You, too, wonder why women can't get along?

Perhaps, though, You look beyond the surface of these women and into their hearts. Maybe the goodness and love You find hidden there keeps You from giving up on us entirely. For in their proudest moments, this same group of bickering, back-stabbing women are capable of giving from their very depths. They can unite and work together in the face of great need or tragedy. They spend long hours knitting mittens for Indian children, organizing a bloodmobile, putting on monthly birthday parties at the rest home. They open their pocketbooks as well as their hearts when someone needs their help. Does this core of unselfishness make You overlook some of our shortcomings?

But, still, Lord, I pray You'll help me and my sisters learn to live in greater harmony with each other. Teach us to better reflect our Christian beliefs in our daily lives. Perhaps if my generation of women make a beginning, my daughter's generation will know the blessing of peace and unity among women.

31

The Double Bed

Nearly every magazine I've read recently carried articles on how to improve sexual relations. The sex act was dissected, analyzed, pulled apart, and put back together in print for anxious readers. And we are anxious about our sex lives. We worry that maybe we don't measure up to the Hollywood standards flashed out at us in technicolor. What we forget is that even memorizing the encyclopedia of sex can't make for satisfying relations if one essential ingredient is missing—love.

FATHER, our world is preoccupied with sex. We are so concerned with technique that we lose the feeling of communion and the expression of love that make sexual relations satisfying and fulfilling. Living together is "in," not "sin," today. Extramarital affairs are so common we scarcely raise our eyebrows at them. We've forgotten the basic morality that is the foundation of Christian faith.

Help me, Father, to avoid the negative influence of society's sexual viewpoints. Remind me that the double bed, the marriage bed my husband and I share, is a place for the giving of ourselves—not a place for bribery, punishment, or criticism. Remind me, too, that while sexual relations are a beautiful expression of love, it is not the only way to express deep feelings. Help me achieve a marriage in which sex plays only a part in a much greater whole.

32

A World of Plastic

"Genuine simulated walnut" the ad for the reproduction antique clock read. "What on earth is genuine simulated walnut?" I asked my husband.

"Plastic," he answered.

"You've got to be kidding. Who would buy a grandfather clock made out of plastic?"

"It's a plastic world," he replied.

And paging through the catalog I realize he is right. Plastic dishes, plastic toys, plastic silverware, plastic flowers, plastic picture frames, even plastic baby bibs! What ever happened to porcelain, silver, walnut, fabric? They seem to have disappeared in this age of plastic.

FATHER, I live in a world of plastics. The things I buy are "simulated" this and "artificial" that. Nothing seems to be true to itself. Nothing is really what it looks like it must be. Rather than enjoying plastic for its own qualities, its plasticness, we try to make it into things it can never be.

People, too, are made of plastic. We've become as simulated and artificial as that grandfather clock. We're afraid to expose our true selves to the world and to You; so we disguise ourselves to look entirely different. Help us, Lord, to erase this plasticness from our lives. Help us to place enough faith in ourselves and in You so we can be what we really are. Teach us how to bring the wood, the porcelain, the silver back into our lives. Give us the courage to say good-bye and good riddance to plastic people!

33

Thoughts on a Thirtieth Birthday

Twelve months have flipped through the calendar again. Twelve times I've pulled off a page thinking how much closer my thirtieth birthday drew. Now it has arrived—that unique day in a woman's life when youth seems so far away in the past and middle age creeping up in the future.

Age thirty is truly a turning point. Suddenly I notice all the questionnaries that have a little box to check labeled "over thirty." I wonder whether I must cancel my subscriptions to the magazines edited for "young women eighteen to thirty." I study myself critically in the mirror, trying to decide if my wardrobe is suitable for my age or if I deserve the scorn fashion editors heap on women who dress younger than their years. Whoa! Is that a gray hair at my temple? Could that little crease near my eyelid mark the beginning of wrinkles?

Overnight I've become very age conscious. I worry about the pretty young girls my husband works alongside. Does he find them more attractive than me? I wonder if my children think I'm old-fashioned and dowdy. These thoughts didn't bother me last year but they plague me now. I rebel against the calendar. I don't want to be thirty!

FATHER, help me accept this birthday and all my future birthdays without tears, without backward glances. Help me remember that even on this thirtieth birthday I am only one day older than I was yesterday morning.

Teach me something worthwhile on this special birthday which bridges decades: teach me to value each day, each month, each year as a gift from Your love. Guide me so I use Your precious gift of time wisely.

Help me, too, to regain my self-confidence. Doubts, fears, worries, if unchecked, can eat away, leaving only a shell of a woman—not the living, loving woman I hope always to be. Like the television commercial, remind me now and then that I'm not getting older, I'm getting better!

34

Thank You for My Friend

"Make new friends but keep the old; one is silver but the other is gold." My best friend is truly a golden part of my life. Over the years we've built up a closeness based on love and trust and a genuine enjoyment of each other's company. Oh, how rare and beautiful is this friendship we have!

We share so much: countless cups of coffee, tears and laughter, rummage sales, hopes and dreams, impromptu lunches, good days and bad. She sees me at my best and at my worst—and accepts me either way. When I'm down, she pours me a cup of coffee and listens to my troubles tumble out. When I'm up, she rejoices with me in my happiness. She's truly a woman without equal, this priceless treasure I call my friend.

FATHER, I thank You for my friend. My life is so much richer for her presence. I pray that You'll watch over her and bless her with an abundance of Your gifts. I pray, too, that I'll never cause her any pain or unhappiness. Don't let angry or thoughtless words ever come between us to break our unique and beautiful bond.

Help me never to take my friend for granted or to forget that friendship is a two-way street. Remind me to give my share to our storehouse of shared memories: a rose from my garden, praise for a job well done, a casserole when she's ill, a shoulder to lean on when she needs it. For surely, Lord, my friend flavors my life on earth with a little taste of heaven.

35

Thy Will Be Done!

Again in church this morning I recited, along with the rest of the congregation, the prayer Your Son Jesus taught us: "Our Father, who art in heaven. . . ." And once again I stumbled over the words that bother me most: "Thy will be done on earth as it is in heaven." *Thy* will be done; not mine, but Yours.

FATHER, I have such difficulty saying these words because I have to struggle to accept them. Of all my many weaknesses, surely You must know that pride is my greatest sin. Humility is not a word in my vocabulary—and it should be. I don't know how to be humble. I don't know how to be subservient. My ego is blown up with hot air. I cannot say, "Thy will be done" because in my heart I really mean *my* will be done!

Help me to trust in You as the Great Planner. Teach me to have faith in Your plan for my life and to accept the way You choose for me without questioning. When my ego tries to convince me that I know what's best for me better than You do, remind me of Your words in Proverbs: "Pride goes before destruction and a haughty spirit before a fall" (16:18). Give me the humility to confess that I am a sinner deserving of hell and that only Your forgiveness and mercy can save me.

36

I've Got to Lose Weight!

It's been a few weeks since I weighed myself; but this morning, when I stepped on the scale, I saw the sum total of all my snacking, nibbling, and just plain unwise eating. The needle pushed up well past its usual resting place, stopping with a quiver in the obese zone.

How I admire those blessed women who can eat all they want and never gain an ounce. Weight has always been a problem for me. I can add five pounds just looking at a hot fudge sundae! In my teen-age years I was just "chubby." Ten pounds more after my first baby and I became "plump." But I can't hide from the brutal truth my mirror reflects back at me today—I'm fat.

LORD, I plead for Your help as I battle the scale. Just look at the beautiful body You gave me, disguised beyond recognition by layers of ugly fat! I'm so ashamed of myself, for I know that this problem is my own fault. I can't blame my glands or my heredity or even You. The cause of my obesity lies within myself; my self-indulgence alone is responsible.

Give me the self-control and fortitude to say no to candy, second helpings, yes, even my favorite food, pizza. Stay with me as the bloom of the first few days of dieting fades and the temptations of food become stronger. And when I reach those horrible plateaus when the scale reads the same morning after morning, give me encouragement to stick to my diet, to reach yet toward my goal.

I confess that I am weak, that without Your help I will surely fail. Please guide me as I begin this long and bumpy journey down the road toward slimness.

37

The Simpler Life for Me?

I read in "back to the earth" magazines of a new breed of woman who has said good-bye to the conveniences of modern living and hello to a rugged, pioneer-style life. Like her grandmother, she cooks on a wood-burning stove, gardens, cans and preserves food, chops wood, and does her family laundry in a tub with a washboard. Her house has no electricity, no central heating or air conditioning, no indoor plumbing. Her husband cares for his land with hand tools, milks goats, and tends beehives. Her children are sometimes taught at home, sometimes in cooperative schools. They play with simple, handmade toys or nature's own toys available just outside the front door.

This life style is so alien to my own—but it fascinates me. I wonder if I could live like this back-to-the-earth sister. Could I give up all my labor-saving devices and creature comforts to carve out a life of self-sufficiency?

LORD, surely You must smile on the efforts of women like these. They are loving and caring for Your land and the creatures You sent to populate it. They do not waste precious natural resources like I often do. They worship You in a simpler, perhaps more personal and honest way than I do.

I don't know, Father, if this is the kind of life You wish me to lead. I don't even know if I *could* do it without resenting the hard work and longing for material objects from my past lifestyle. Is a pioneer life of self-sufficiency a step backward or a step forward—or maybe a stride in each direction? Help me resolve my doubts and know in my heart Your plan for me and my family. Let us know if this is the road of life You wish us to follow.

38

Thinking About Death

She was only thirty-five, a wife and mother, a choir director and career woman. She had no way of knowing that death approached—that the brakes on the bus would fail and a destroying mass of metal would hurtle toward her. One minute she was alive and happy; the next, departed, leaving family and friends to grieve a death that came too soon.

LORD, the death of another brings an awareness of my own temporary existence on earth. A lifetime can be so short and so abruptly ended. What can I hope to accomplish in mine? What have I accomplished already? Have my husband, children, family, and friends benefited from my presence among them? Help me today to assess my life as a Christian woman. Show me where I'm lacking—where I've delayed, put off, omitted good intentions thinking I could do it tomorrow. Impress on me that I may not have a tomorrow; so I should make the most of today.

Help me, too, to find meaning in this death of a young woman. It seems such a tragic, senseless waste that I confess I can't find Your purpose in it. Won't You provide Your strength to the family left behind? They grieve her loss and must be searching, as I am, for a reason to explain death. Comfort them that they can go on with life even in the face of death.

39

The Foolishness of Fashion

Again this season, as I go through my closet, I am discarding good, wearable clothing because it's not "in fashion." Long skirts I can, and have, shortened when hemlines rose. But what can I do with all these miniskirts and short dresses that were so fashionable a year or two ago, now that the hemline has dropped down to the knee again? The shoes with pointed toes, all the peg-legged pants, jackets with narrow lapels, and blouses that weren't made of permanently pressed fabric have already gone the way of the Goodwill box in past seasons.

Fashion is such a foolish, fickle master to follow; yet I am as much a slave to the whims of designers and fashion editors as any woman. I, too, have spent money I couldn't really afford on fads and favorites of the times. Like many of my sisters, I've worn garments that weren't becoming to my figure or suitable to my lifestyle, shoes that have pinched my toes and caused bunions, colors that made my face look like flour. Why are we women so willing to become slaves of fashion?

LORD, You have told us not to worry about material things, that You would provide. "Consider the lilies of the field, how they grow; they neither toil nor spin; yet I tell you, even Solomon in all his glory was not arrayed like one of these. But if God so clothes the grass of the field, which today is alive and tomorrow is thrown into the oven, will he not much more clothe you?" (Matt. 6:28-30). Help me to remember these words as I sort my closet. Remind me of them again whenever I shop for clothing.

If I must discard usable clothing, let me look first to what can be salvaged. Are there buttons, zippers, material to go into a patchwork quilt which could be saved and reused? Could I alter a dress or cut it off and make a skirt? Could the too-tight slacks be cut down to make a pair of pants for one of my children? Give my conscience a twinge before I toss anything into the garbage can. Remind me that not all Your children are blessed with the abundance I enjoy. Thank You for the riches You've showered on my family which enables us to have packed closets—and help me remember not to waste and squander Your blessings by being a slave to fashion.

40

Kicking the Dryer Doesn't Help!

I'm just going to sit down and have a cup of coffee. All of my fretting and fuming hasn't gotten me anywhere. Maybe if I try to forget about it for awhile, put my mind on something else, I'll do better when I try again.

My problem is very simple. Any three-year-old could take one look at the situation and come up with a solution. Two of the three screws which hold the drum on my clothes dryer in position have worked out. I found the screws (thanks for small favors!) so all I have to do is replace them. An easy quick little task. Except that the holes in the drum won't line up with those in the dryer body. After an hour with my head in the dryer, screwdriver in hand, I'm totally frustrated. Banging on the top of the dryer with the screwdriver didn't help. Crying didn't accomplish a thing. Maybe a cup of coffee will relieve these feelings of fury and futility.

FATHER, I am so easily frustrated. Perhaps You have given me too easy a life. Maybe I can't handle little setbacks because I've never had to work long and hard at accomplishing anything, or known deprivation, or battled against bigotry and prejudice. Two screws falling out of my dryer is such a trivial problem that I'm truly ashamed of the blind rage I feel.

Help me, Lord, to deal calmly with life's little frustrations, to keep my cool, as my kids would say. Teach me that there comes a time when I must stand back from my problems, look at them with a new eye, and then make a fresh start toward a solution. Remind me of the tremendous frustration Your Son Jesus experienced in His life here on earth, culminating in that final frustration as He hung on the cross. How minor my difficulty with the clothes dryer becomes when viewed in that perspective!

Now—back to that dangling drum.

41

Patchwork Quilt

"You've got to get rid of all those fabric scraps," my husband said firmly, viewing the corner of the basement where shelves were lined with boxes, and bags stuffed full of leftover material.

Being a person who saves anything which might still be usable, I replied in my most practical voice, "I'm planning to make a patchwork quilt some-day."

"Then get started on it right now!"

So here I sit with 940 small squares of fabric to join. Gay ginghams and calicos, pretty prints, stripes, and plaids wink back at me. That nice vague "someday" has arrived. I wish now I'd given all my material scraps to the lady down the road who makes Barbie doll clothes!

FATHER, I am so much like a tiny scrap of left-over material. On my own I am really not very valuable. My use to You and others is limited by my human faults and failings. Remind me occasionally, as You did today while I was working on the quilt, that beauty, size, and strength come from many scraps joining together into a greater whole. Teach me to join with my fellow church members, neighbors, family and friends to serve You better. Let me be one small square in that glorious patchwork quilt made up of Your faithful servants here on earth.

42

The Fire

I slept right through the sirens, fire whistle, and commotion. It wasn't until the next morning that I saw what fire had done to my friend's home. A smoldering pile of black rubble was all that remained.

What does one say to someone who has lost everything? It's a shock to lose the replaceables like clothing and furniture, but, even more heartbreaking is the loss of the irreplaceables like photo albums, children's "presents," and the heirloom cedar chest that was handed down through the family for generations. "I'm sorry" seems so inadequate.

I tried to comfort her, but it was she who comforted me. "Don't feel so bad," she said. "We didn't lose so much." I stared at the ashes which had once been a home. She must have read my unspoken question for she explained gently, "I still have my husband and child. Isn't that what really counts?"

LORD, I pray today for this family who has lost so much to fire but who has the wisdom to know how much more they might have lost. Console them in their time of turmoil and help them to rebuild not only a house, but a home.

Help me to learn from my young friend's strength and courage. Help me to absorb the kind of values and priorities which put life over possessions, gratitude for what I have above bitterness over what I've lost or been denied. Let this fire mark the beginning of new spiritual growth and a greater awareness and appreciation of what is truly important in my life.

43

Forgiveness

I'm sure my friend didn't mean to hurt my feelings. Maybe she really did forget about the invitation I'd extended for Saturday night. It could have just slipped her mind so that when another invitation came, she accepted without thinking of me at all. I know I shouldn't feel so badly about it. But I'd planned and prepared for the evening all week. My house was cleaned, food and drink set out, and they never arrived. When I finally called to see what was holding them up, the baby sitter said they'd left for a party an hour ago.

FATHER, my friend has apologized for forgetting and I accepted her apology. Now I ask that You'll help me find real forgiveness in my heart. Help me not only to forgive, but also to forget. Remind me of all the kind and thoughtful things she's done for me over the years. Let me concentrate on the blessing of this friendship and erase this and all past grievances from my memory. In the prayer You gave us we ask You "to forgive us our trespasses as we forgive those who trespass against us." Help me to find the same forgiveness for my friend that You find for me when I come to You with my sins.

44

Loneliness

The house seems so quiet now that the children are tucked into their beds. I turned on the television but it doesn't fill the void left by my husband's absence. Another meeting for him, another lonely evening for me.

Perhaps if I had a job outside my home, I wouldn't have the feeling that I've lost contact with the world. No one to talk to all day and now no one with me to share the evening. I'm hungry for company. Loneliness is as gnawing and painful as a toothache.

FATHER, how selfish I am to complain of loneliness when You are always ready to share an evening with me. But I've been so busy feeling sorry for myself that I've forgotten to invite You into my life. My heart was so closed up with self-pity that there was no room for You to enter.

Help me to conquer this loneliness I feel. This is the time to take a long bubble bath, to do my nails and give myself a facial, to start reading my new murder mystery—to do all those things I complain I can't find time to do. Remind me, Father, that alone and lonely don't have to be synonymous. Help me learn how to savour my hours of aloneness without feeling lonely.